Response Activities

ELL
Grade 4

Harcourt School Publishers

www.harcourtschool.com

Response Activities

ELL

Grade 4

⟨⟨Harcourt School Publishers

www.harcourtschool.com

Printed in the United States of America

ISBN 10 0-15-358786-5

ISBN 13 978-0-15-358786-3

1 2 3 4 5 6 7 8 9 10   947   16 15 14 13 12 11 10 09 08 07

Summer Fun

What is your favorite summer sport?

1. Write about your favorite summer sport.

2. Draw yourself playing the sport.

Under the Sea

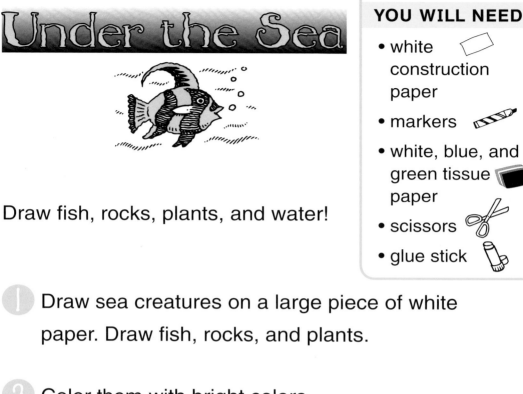

Draw fish, rocks, plants, and water!

YOU WILL NEED

- white construction paper
- markers
- white, blue, and green tissue paper
- scissors
- glue stick

1. Draw sea creatures on a large piece of white paper. Draw fish, rocks, and plants.

2. Color them with bright colors.

3. Cut white, blue, and green tissue paper. Glue pieces on to look like water.

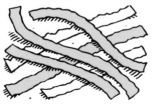

Grade 4, Lesson 30

Under the Sea

Baseball Poster

YOU WILL NEED
- paper
- pen
- colored pencils

Draw a poster to show baseball equipment.

1 Draw something you use to play baseball.

2 Under the drawing, write what it is.

3 Tell how you use it to play baseball.

Animals on the Wall

Make a cave wall drawing.

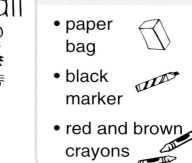

YOU WILL NEED

- paper bag
- black marker
- red and brown crayons

1 Crumple a paper bag many times. Then flatten it.

2 Draw an animal. Draw dark lines.

3 Rub red and brown crayons around the picture to make it look like a rock.

4 Under the drawing, write the name of the animal.

Grade 4, Lesson 29   **The Great Land of Alaska**

Come to a Picnic!

YOU WILL NEED

- white construction paper
- scissors
- crayons
- pencil

Plan a picnic for your family!

1. Draw a circle. Cut it out. This is a plate!

2. Draw the foods you would eat at a picnic.

3. Turn the plate over. Draw your family at a picnic.

Enjoy Your Vacation!

YOU WILL NEED

- paper
- pen
- markers

Help your friend decide where to go on vacation.

1 Draw a good place to go on vacation.

Eiffel Tower

2 At the bottom of the paper, write a letter to your friend:

Dear _____,

The best place to have a vacation is _____

because _____.

Your Friend,

_____

Grade 4, Lesson 28

It's Vacation Time!

A Postcard from Chinatown

Write a postcard to a friend!

1 Draw Chinatown on the index card.

2 On the back of the card, write a letter to a friend.

Dear _____,

I am in Chinatown! I see _____.

I like _____.

Your friend,

_____

My City

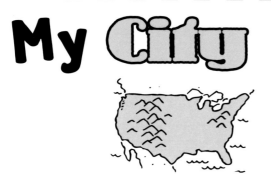

Tell about your city and state.

1 Draw your city or town. If it is too big to draw, draw your favorite part of your city or town.

2 Name your city and state.

3 Write where your state is. Is it in the Northeast, Southeast, Midwest, West, or Southwest United States? Or do you live in Alaska or Hawaii?

It's a Holiday!

YOU WILL NEED

- construction paper
- markers or colored pencils
- pen or pencil

Make a card about your favorite holiday.

1. Fold a piece of paper in half. This is a card.

2. On the outside, write a holiday name. Draw something that happens during the holiday.

3. On the inside, write what people do on the holiday.

Museum

YOU WILL NEED
- drawing paper
- markers

What kind of museum would you like to visit? Make an ad for that museum.

1. Name your museum.

2. Draw a picture in the middle of your ad. Draw objects that would be in the museum.

3. At the bottom, tell about one or two special objects. Tell why they are at the museum.

A Pioneer's Story

YOU WILL NEED
- pen
- paper

Write a story about American pioneers!

1. Imagine you moved west as a pioneer.

2. Write a letter to a friend or family member. Tell the person about your trip. Use details from the story.

3. Decorate your letter.

A Visit to Williamsburg

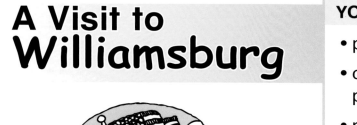

 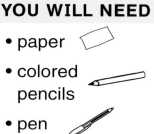
What would you do in Williamsburg, Virginia?

1. Think about the story. Imagine your teacher said that your class would visit Williamsburg.

2. What parts of Williamsburg seemed interesting? Write a letter to your teacher. Tell your teacher things you would like to do.

Four Seasons

YOU WILL NEED

- white construction paper
- colored pencils

Show how seasons change.

1 Fold your paper in half. Fold your paper in half again. Now you have four squares!

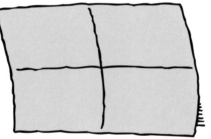

2 Write a season in each square: *fall, winter, spring, summer*.

3 Draw how a tree looks in each season.

4 Write something you do in each season.

Grade 4, Lesson 7   Grandpa and I, All Year Long

Florida Collage

YOU WILL NEED

- construction paper
- old magazines
- scissors
- glue

Create a collage of images of Florida.

1. Look in magazines. Find pictures of animals, flowers, trees, and other images of Florida.

2. Glue the pictures to construction paper.

3. On the back, finish the sentence:

   In Florida, I would like to see _____.

Computer 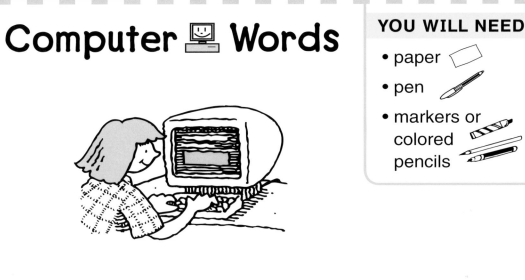 Words

What do you know about computers?

1. Draw a computer on a piece of paper. Be sure to include a monitor, keyboard, mouse, and CD-ROM.

2. Label the parts of the computer.

3. Tell how you can use a computer.

Your Own Money

YOU WILL NEED

• colored construction paper

• colored pencils

Make money for an imaginary land.

1 Draw a rectangle on construction paper.

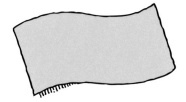

2 In the middle, draw your face. Write your name under the drawing.

3 Decorate your money. Draw things about your imaginary land. The money must show things important to you!

A Special Day

What is your favorite family tradition?

1. Think about a family tradition. Draw what you do during the tradition.

2. Under the drawing, tell about the tradition.

My Home

YOU WILL NEED

- paper
- pen
- pencil

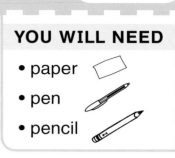

Tell about where you live.

1. Draw a picture of your home. Do you live in a city, suburb, or on a ranch? Do you live somewhere else?

2. Finish the sentences:

   I live in a _____ .

   I get to school by _____ .

   After school, I like to _____ .

At the National Park

Tell what you do at a national park.

1 Draw a tree with branches on green paper.

2 On the branches of the tree, finish the sentence:

At a national park, I can _____.

3 At the bottom, finish the sentence:

At a national park, people should not _____.

A Pet for Me

YOU WILL NEED
- paper
- pen
- markers or colored pencils

Write about a pet you would like.

1 Choose a pet you would like. It can be any pet you can think of!

2 Finish the sentences:

I would like this pet because _____.

I would take care of it by _____.

Crafty Creatures

YOU WILL NEED

- construction paper
- colored pencils or markers

Show how an animal finds food and stays safe.

1 Draw an animal.

2 Finish the sentences:

My animal's shelter is a_____.

It eats _____.

It stays safe from predators by _____.

Dust for Fingerprints

YOU WILL NEED

- plastic objects
- powder
- drawing paper

Dust for fingerprints like a real detective!

1. Touch one of the plastic objects. Make sure you press your fingers on it.

2. Put a little powder on the object. Look for the fingerprints.

3. On drawing paper, draw what you see.

To the MOUNTAINS

YOU WILL NEED

- brown and blue construction paper
- markers
- chalk
- scissors
- index cards

Draw a mountain. Then tell about it!

1. Draw a mountain on brown paper. Cut it out.

2. Glue your mountain to blue paper.

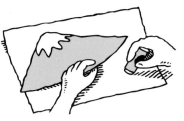

3. Draw trees on your mountains. Use chalk to draw snow.

4. On the index card, write about going to the mountains. Glue the index card to the picture.

That's My Dinner!

YOU WILL NEED
- drawing paper
- markers

Where does your food come from?

1. Draw two circles on your paper.

2. Write **Garden** in one circle. Write **Farm** in the other.

3. Put these foods into the right circles: *milk, apples, eggs, lettuce, tomatoes, yogurt*. Add other foods that fit in the circles.

Save the Forests!

Make a book about forest fires.

1. Fold two sheets of white construction paper in half.

2. Staple them together to make a book.

3. Draw a forest on the front. Write a title for the book.

4. On each page, write one cause of forest fires.

   Draw a picture to show the cause.

What I Can Do!

YOU WILL NEED
- lined paper
- pen
- markers

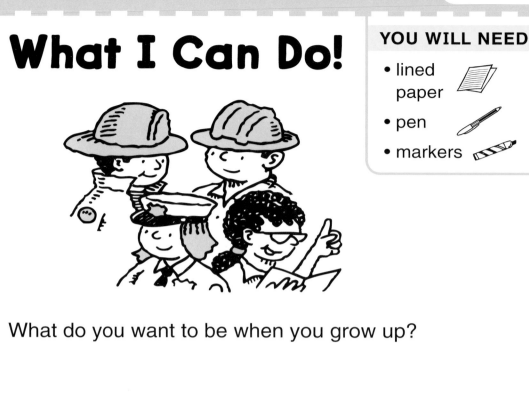

What do you want to be when you grow up?

1) At the top of your paper, write jobs you could do.

2) Choose one job you like. Draw yourself on the job.

My Favorite Season

Tell about your favorite season.

1. Draw your favorite season.

2. Finish the sentence:

This is my favorite season because _____.

Draw Your Story

YOU WILL NEED

- drawing paper
- colored pencils
- pen

Tell a story about your life!

1 Draw 4 boxes on paper. Number the boxes 1–4.

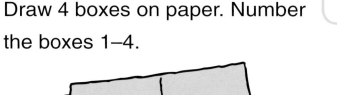

2 Think of a story to tell about your life. Draw the story in four parts. Draw one part in each box.

3 Under each drawing, tell what happened.

Coral Reef Poster

YOU WILL NEED

- drawing paper
- markers

Draw a poster about the coral reef.

1. At the top of your paper, write "Coral Reef" in big red letters.

2. Draw animals that live near the coral reef.

3. Write the name of each animal in your language and in English.

That's Better...

Invent something new!

1. Choose an object.

umbrella		pen		lamp	
television		glasses		skateboard	
backpack		shoes		mirror	

2. Draw how you would make it better.

3. Write how you would make it better under your drawing.